The Upsilon Factor

A Framework for Societal Decision-Making Based on Logic and Reason Without Resorting to Moral Assertion

ISVAHL INAJ

Version 1.0

Copyright © 2022, Isvahl Inaj.

All Rights Reserved.

ISBN (Hardcover): 979-8-9856136-0-5
ISBN (Amazon E-book): 979-8-9856136-1-2

www.isvahlinaj.com, Official Website.
(Backup - https://linktr.ee/isvahlinaj)

Hardcover Published by Gatekeeper Press
2167 Stringtown Rd., Suite 109
Columbus, OH 43123-2989
The cover design, interior formatting, typesetting, and editorial work for this book are entirely the product of the author. Gatekeeper Press did not participate in and is not responsible for any aspect of these elements.

Dedication

There is a resonance I feel with the conjecture that we are all of us searching, always. I know of two things for which human searches: meaning, and truth. For those who search for meaning, it may well be that love gives them meaning. But for those who seek truth, there are no answers in love. The answers lay in insight. Had I to choose between experiencing and understanding love, I would, perhaps regrettably, accept the pain of never experiencing love for the possibility of understanding it. This book is dedicated to my one true love, Insight.

- Isvahl

Contents

Preface	6
An Analogy	9
Goal Of This Work	9
What Is A Belief?	10
Foundational Beliefs and Assumptions In This Work	10
Assumption A: The Existence of the Universe and Our Consciousnesses	10
Assumption B: The Fidelity of Logic	11
An Acknowledged Limitation: Intuitive Universality	11
A Framework To Assess Abandonability Of Beliefs	12
On Morals (Row E)	14
On Empathy (Row D)	15
Variable Definitions	20
Pleasure and Pain	20
Direct vs Indirect Experience	21
Secondary Empathetic Suffering	21
Self-Empathy	22
Summations of Empathetic Suffering	22
Additional Empathy-Weighting Caveats	23
Empathy-Weighted Joy	23
Parameterizing Empathetic Weighting	23
How Orthogonal Are Joy and Suffering?	23
A Note On Derivational Approach	25
The Snowball	28
Omega: The Threshold of Intolerable Suffering	28
Alpha: The Maintenance Of Will To Survive	29
Upsilon: The Reduction of Empathy-Weighted Suffering	29
From Binary to Gradated; Hierarchical to Interactive	29
Upsilon Definition	30
Zeta: The Pursuit of Joy	31
Summarizing All Four Factors	32
Trading Off Upsilon and Zeta	33
A Deeper Examination Of Upsilon / Zeta Trade Offs	36

Nuance of Distractibility	39
Why The Focus on Upsilon?	**41**
Applying the Upsilon Factor	**42**
Three-Person Universe	42
Empathy-Weighting Matrix	42
The First Constitution	43
Crab-Induced Blindness and Consumption	43
Consuming Crabs Recreationally	44
Consuming Crabs Medicinally	46
Hypothetical Disagreement	50
Summary	**51**
Naturalism vs Consensus-ism	51
References	**52**
Further Reading	**54**

Preface

I humbly suggest that you not read the preface until you have read the rest of this work. However, knowledge of the information in this preface may be useful context when interpreting this work.

Ever since I was a young child, I began asking myself deep questions, like "why did I have no say in whether I exist, and on what terms I exist?". The popular concept of original position posits that when a society is created, it be on such terms that anyone who could become a participant in that society should be content to be subject to the laws that apply to any random participant in that society.

For example, if a society's design entailed that robbers would be imprisoned, then anyone theoretically given a blindfold upon creation of the society and told that were they to become a robber they would be imprisoned, should be allowed to block that society's creation if they were not okay with that contract. Yet we are not actually given this opportunity at birth. We are not invited to a roundtable to discuss what our existence on this planet will entail, and by what rules of society we must engage, in order to determine whether we feel comfortable entering existence with the parents and societies we forcibly inherit.

Oppression begins with our birth. Our progenitors have absolute physical power over us -- the ability to mandate where we urinate or defecate and what we eat. We have no choice or faculty to relocate to our own home with our own rules, both because of most countries' laws, and because we would have to earn such a home by serving an oppressor who previously owned it (such as by working to earn capital that could be exchanged for it). Importantly, we never had any choice of whether to accept these conditions before we were born.

In most modern governments, our incapacity to live freely extends to schooling. This could be considered outsourced oppression on behalf of the parents (e.g. in the case of private school), or governmental oppression in the sense that there are frequently legal requirements to attend public or private schools for a minimum number of years. In that environment, the language you use, the activities you spend your time on, all are subject to the dictates of a teacher who has immense power over your choices. As a student, you were not involved in designing the rules of your school curriculum, have little-to-no franchise in their governance, and have no reasonable method to opt-out of them.

As adults, we largely look past the oppression of our youth, but we still live in societies where rules are made based on the principles, beliefs, and values of members in that society. In democratic contexts, these are generally the consensus-based agreements on societal regulations that govern human conduct. Often we have more agency in legislative design as adults than we do as children, though not necessarily in all societies.

Many philosophical works have been written on the principles that underlie such legislative design. For the most part, they all start from baseline assumptions of deontological "rights", "wrongs", "shoulds", "oughts" and "ought nots". "Thou shalt not kill," for example. Yet there is no epistemological truth to cognitivist norms that can be proven through rigorous scientific means. And the most common alternative to arbitrary moral dictums tends to be nihilism, which in its most extreme form can approach questioning existence itself.

This work acknowledges that all humans have an entire spectrum of ideas along which they can allocate belief. A human can choose to believe that "thou shall not kill" is an axiomatic fact of the universe. But then when confronted with trolley problems and questions around situations like euthenasia and abortion, this principle in practice starts becoming qualified, ("thou shall not kill except when…"), instead of a deeper questioning of whether the original dictum itself is actually and provably true in any manner. When we build societies from illogical and unprovable presumptions about "rights" and "wrongs", we end up confronting conflicts between subjective evaluations of these so-called moral truths, and the ability to build consensus between all humans begins to diminish. Ideally, a social contract could be designed between humans that acknowledges only that which is factual, and limits presumptions to those critically necessary to enable cooperation.

What I attempt to accomplish in this work is to set out the least common denominators of beliefs and optimization functions that, when applied to the design of a society of humans, can congrue with our observable human neurological functioning and lead to outcomes that are most desirable to the individual neurological consciousnesses that might make up a human society under a premise of original position.

This work is only a proposal. And importantly it is an exploration that might spawn improvements and variations -- a "version 1," to use technology management parlance. And this work both builds from divined assumptions that might be unpalatable to nihilists, as well as my own personal introspection which may not reflect the intuition of all other humans with perfect accuracy, or perhaps any accuracy at all. However, it aims to minimize those assumptions to only the barest necessary to allow for any framework of social cohesion to occur that could in theory enable communal consent to governance design. One could think of this work as, *"maximizing the ratio of social consensus-buildability to dogmatic presumption"*.

As such I will use the first person pronoun "i" in much of this writing, to make clear that this entire treatise derives from the projection of my own intuition about my reasoning, to that of all other humans. I will describe later why I am comfortable proposing such a projection and extrapolation, in the interest of propagating this template for thinking about social optimization functions. I may at times extend the pronoun "i" to "we", to reference the imaginative alter-ego of the reader who puts themselves in the shoes of a person who already believes in my arguments, such that the reader might find it easier to foresee a path from their status quo worldview to the ideas proposed in this work.

Lastly, where possible I will attempt to provide references to neurological research that supports the conclusions drawn about human psychology that form my aforementioned intuitions.

Well then, let us begin!

An Analogy

Imagine you are writing a book on plants. Your readers are to be measured by their performance on a standardized biology exam, and your aim is to raise their scores.

Suppose you are only able to re-use complete sentences from other books to write this book. When this approach is taken, the average score of your student readers turns out to be X.

Now suppose you are allowed to use individual words from other books (including the dictionary), and combine those words into new sentences. Presumably the readers in this second situation would score above an average of X, as you can introduce and frame new ideas in a way they would find comprehensible.

Imagine you could go one step further, and use any letter or alphanumeric character in the English language to create your book, enabling you to coin new terms of art where applicable to express your concepts. That intuitively would lead to the most optimal performance by readers of your book.

When thinkers can operate on the finest granules of a system, they can produce the most optimal output.

Goal Of This Work

The goal of this work is to propose a social construct, called the Upsilon Factor, that can produce the highest degree of societal consensus, while requiring the lowest common denomination of shared human beliefs as input. The finest granules of belief, if you will.

The benefit of such a construct is that it can be used by humans, like government policy makers, to reach a consensus decision that optimizes for those shared beliefs, eschewing the tax imposed by having to barter around incompatible beliefs between decision-makers.

The distillation of these lowest common denominators, and the consensus-building formula that build on them, aim to leverage our best understanding of neuroscience, and complement it with logic and introspective intuition.

What Is A Belief?

A synthesis of the various dictionary definitions of "belief" might be, a conviction that something is true or exists.

Since our goal requires isolating a lowest common denomination of shared human beliefs, we might start by proposing that among the universe of possible beliefs a human may hold (from "i exist" to "my home is haunted"), this lowest denomination includes a core set of beliefs unabandonable by any human, complemented perhaps by an additional set of conceivably abandonable beliefs, that are requisite for participating decision-makers to even desire any consensus (lest this endeavor be bereft of need).

However, in order to negotiate these two properties of beliefs -- abandonability and criticality to motivating a desire for human consensus -- we must rely on constructs, like reason, that are beliefs themselves. While it could be the case that there are members of the species who do not hold any such foundational beliefs, without making certain "axiomatic" presumptions, this work could not progress. I aim to minimize those presumptions as much as imaginably possible.

So we will start by exploring foundational beliefs, stating our assumptions, and then reason through additional beliefs to negotiate their abandonability and/or their criticality to the desire of human consensus.

Foundational Beliefs and Assumptions In This Work

Assumption A: The Existence of the Universe and Our Consciousnesses

Nihilists will question existence itself. I cannot come up with a clear and rigorous logical proof of the existence of everything.

However I do find myself believing the universe, and our consciousnesses, exist (i.e. they are "real" in the colloquial sense). And so while there is a possibility neither exists, this entire work is premised on the belief and presumption they both do. I can only hope this foundational assertion will not turn away the reader. Nihilists may still derive value from this work, by considering it a treatise that explores decision-making possibilities conditional on the predicate that the universe and our consciousnesses exist.

Assumption B: The Fidelity of Logic

My second assumption is that the laws of logic hold "true". Those laws include DeMorgan's laws of logic and form the plane of reason undergirding the entire work you are reading. Once again, I cannot prove that logical deductions confer truth and recognize there are known (including mathematical) paradoxes in the universe arising purely from logical manipulation and observable fact.

But also again, my observations of the universe are consistent with the laws of logic, and I opt (perhaps "religiously") to believe in logic. Where paradoxes arise from pure logical reasoning around observable facts, this work will aim to address those paradoxes head on. As with existence, the nihilist may derive value from this work by considering it an exploration conditioned on the predicate of logical integrity.

There is a corollary to this assumption of logical integrity, which is that all humans who believe in and follow the integrity of logic can deduce the same conclusions as this work does. There is ample evidence [1] that most humans are naturally convinced by logical deduction and that reason forms a common plane of understanding between communicating individuals. That assumption again leads to a wide scope of applicability of this work to the minds and societies of thinking people.

An Acknowledged Limitation: Intuitive Universality

There is a key limitation in the process of this work. Namely, I draw from introspective cognitive assessments of my own neurological manifestation, and I make the vast generalization that others may find my reasoning compelling on the basis that most individuals share this same broad neural platform. There is much empirical evidence that our similarities as humans, even psychologically, far outweigh our differences. And that well over 99% of our DNA is identical. And countless studies have shown similar neural reactions to various stimuli that constitute fear, disgust, dopamine release, and other basic emotions among people.

This context convinces me that, within a range of customizable parameters, most readers will usually arrive at the same conclusions I do when following this work's logic and confronting various thought experiments that test our decision-making processes.

A Framework To Assess Abandonability Of Beliefs

Human brains are wired to be predisposed to (i.e. frequently adopt) a range of beliefs and feelings. This range covers a spectrum of feelings from those which seem impossible to abandon, to those which we commonly abandon as part of maturity. Examples of beliefs and feelings across this spectrum are illustrated in the chart below, ranging from the most "core" (least abandonable) on the bottom, to the most commonly abandoned on the top:

Table 1: Predisposed Beliefs

Predisposition	Example of Manifestation
I. Entitlement *[Most Abandonable]*	"Any object I am playing with is mine and not to be shared with anyone else." [2]
H. Magic	"When a magician pulls a rabbit out of a hat that rabbit magically appeared out of thin air, and was not actually hidden in a compartment inside of the hat or otherwise placed in the hat through sleight of hand." [3]
G. Reflexive Violence	"If I believe another person has orally insulted me, that person deserves to be punched, and so I shall punch that person" [4]
F. Racism	"If an Asian American applies for a job they must be better at the quantitative aspects of the work than the African American applying for the same job, and if both are trying out for a basketball team, the African American will lead to better team performance if picked than the Asian American." [5]
E. Morals	"Lying is inherently wrong." [6, 7, 8]
D. Empathy	"When I see a person get hit by a car in front of me, I wince in vicarious pain" [9]
C. Logical Integrity	"If x implies y, then not y implies not x" [10, 11, 12]
B. Existence	"The universe and my consciousness exist" [1]
A. Survival *[Least Abandonable]*	"I must keep breathing." [13]

Note: Rows (C) and (B) correspond to the assumptions already detailed earlier in this work

In the above list, the bottom row "(A) Survival" is the least abandonable trait of our psyches. It affects even those who question existence, because survival drive is subconscious (and because we take existence to be axiomatic). It would take a massive amount of determination to willfully prevent our 'reptilian' brain centers (our cerebella, for example) to cease coordinating the neuromuscular orchestration of terminating involuntary movements, like inhaling and exhaling oxygen or the maintaining the beating of the heart, to the point of death. For example, even among those who attempt suicide, lethality typically requires a method that cannot be easily reversed mid-attempt [14]. The failure rate of a purely unassisted method like sustained and purely willful apnea would be, intuitively, very high. Corroboratingly, voluntary apnea is an empirically insignificant (perhaps even non-existent) contributor to the volume of suicide deaths [Ibid].

It stands to reason that most human beings are unlikely to be able to cognitively de-program the reflexive will to survive from their subconsciousness. While there are cases of people on their deathbeds choosing to no longer fight for survival, and of course people who lose the will to *live* (suiciders), we consider both of those to be reactions to involuntary circumstances, as opposed to a situation where a person consciously *desired* to lose the will to live. This work proposes that there is an implicit desire to sustain the will to live that is contained within the concept of "will to survive," even if that will to live itself is often abandoned. Introspectively, my brain finds it impossible to wish for the universe to be such that I find I have lost my will to live, and I can only take that inclination to be a consequence of human survival instinct.

In contrast, one of the top rows, "(H) Magic," is routinely abandoned by most educated and logical adults. Even when an adult cannot immediately explain a magician's method for pulling a rabbit out of a hat or guessing a card randomly chosen from a deck, experienced adult observers typically assume that there must have been a sleight of hand at play, as opposed to believing the magician was actually demonstrating supernatural prowess.

A more mundane example of this abandonment of superstition is the development of cognitive "object permanence" in children. When an object (say, a toy) is temporarily obscured from a child's view by a block of wood, the child at a young age stops seeking that toy, as they believe it ceases to exist. An older child however, will acknowledge that the toy still does exist. This childhood abandonment of the belief that the toy actually vanishes upon obscuration, exemplifies how the predispositions we hold as youths are not always accurate.

Similarly, the assumptions in Rows "(G) Reflexive Violence" and "(I) Entitlement" in the above chart are routinely abandoned by most children, as they grow and adopt concepts like sharing and ownership, and embrace alternatives to resorting to reflexive violence as the only optional response to any who offend them.

An example of a predisposition that is abandoned by some but not all humans, and to varying extents, is one of the middle rows "(F) Racism". Heuristic generalizations that people form of others, based on superficial (often visual) clusters like race and influenced by in/out-group dynamics, are natural and frequent prejudices that have been demonstrated throughout history across human cultures [15, 16]. Evolutionary psychology suggests that the benefit of such heuristic simplifications is that they enable quick decision-making without expending cognitive load to process each individual unit in a decision (where the "unit" in this example is an individual being assessed, e.g. the job applicant in the chart's examples). In fact, it may even be statistically true that these heuristics are reasonably accurate predictions: a survey of Asian American and African American adults, assessed for their quantitative and athletic accomplishments, may reveal a significant statistical difference between the medians of the two clusters as evaluated on the level to which each capability has manifested.

However, many of us choose to disabuse ourselves of reliance or bias based on these racist heuristics because the cost of the inaccurate over-generalization to individuals across the population, and the potential misattribution of 100% of differences in manifest capability to nature vs nurture, contradicts our objectives. Every minority not given a chance at an activity because they were never even fully evaluated based on statistical over-projection, serves to not only harm outliers but discourage that minority group as a whole from pursuing the activity, and propel homogeneity in social groupings which can reduce biodiversity and increase intergroup conflict, alienation and inequity.

People may choose to abandon certain notions with which they are born, but this abandonment does not invalidate that the predispositions exist. Humans still err toward generalizations and heuristics writ large, but many humans simply choose to consciously "silence" certain generalizations. Even these silencing actions can be incomplete. For example, research has indicated that implicit racial associations can linger in adults' amygdalas even after making robust efforts to "de-program" their tendency toward racist generalizations [17]. But conscious behavior *predicated* on the implicit fear-conditioning response of the amygdala can be attenuated. Said differently, we can abandon the cognitive credence we give to instinctual, subconscious predispositions like racial prejudices.

On Morals (Row E)

Row "(E) Morals" is an instrumental row for this analysis. Much of philosophy has accepted moral dogmas as truths on the basis that almost all humans and all cultures "subconsciously feel" these moral impulses and they tend to be similar across civilizations.

Cognitivism is the branch of philosophy that assigns truth value to normative or moral statements, like "lying is inherently wrong". However, I argue that much like racist generalizations and superstitious beliefs, the predisposition humans have toward believing in moral truths is simply another heuristic that evolved to simplify decision-making. Similarly to racism, moral conviction is a predisposition that can often exacerbate interpersonal harm and human suffering [18]. (We will define the notion of suffering and why it matters for social decision-making in more detail later).

It is easy to see why a species might evolve to have a heuristic predisposition against "sins" like murder or deceit, given that social harmony likely leads to better group-level reproductive outcomes. But belief does not confer truth. Because moral axioms are not observable (the belief is observable but the moral itself is not), it cannot be scientifically proven that murder is "wrong" (nor can the entire concept of "wrongness" be proven to exist or be scientifically defined).

The diversity in attitudes toward murder also reinforces the notion that this moral predisposition is, essentially, an oversimplified heuristic distillation of empathetic and altruistic impulses (Row D, analyzed later in this work). A person can claim "killing humans is wrong," but then abortion, euthenasia, survivalist carnivorism, and capital punishment, all contradict that belief, and their moral valences lack unaniminity across observers. Further, moral virtues often conflict with each other, as is the case when deliberating whether lying (a "sin"), to save someone from murder, is "less sinful" than allowing a murder to commence. The classic conundrum demonstrating this conflict is the imagined scenario where a murderer calls you to ask whether your neighbor, whom the murderer is seeking to kill and who is hiding in your house, is hiding in your house.

Because morals are neither observable facts, nor enjoy unanimous consensus in their substance, I submit that we can best build a platform for human cooperation by wholly eschewing our predisposition toward moral beliefs. This proposition forms a grounding foundation for this work. While, similar to racism, this "unlearning" process may not always be neurally comprehensive, the more societies can consciously cooperate in terms of observable and undisputed truths and facts, the more likely this society is to be able to cooperate at all.

As mentioned earlier, the goal of this work is to develop a framework that maximizes the ratio of social consensus-buildability to dogmatic presumptiveness. Accordingly, and importantly, **this work eschews all moral faith**.

On Empathy (Row D)

Row "(D) Empathy" is a crucial row to dissect for the exercise of deriving the Upsilon Factor. My analysis here will draw very heavily from introspection.

My self-observation is that I feel empathy. Empathy is defined by the Oxford Dictionary as "the ability to understand and share the feelings of another." For the sake of this work, we will more narrowly focus on the aspect of empathy that is the ability to feel pain when apprehending the pain of another.

I will state that I am less sure how much pleasure I truly feel when apprehending the pleasure of another than I am about my vicarious feelings of pain. I am aware that mirror neurons cause humans to smile upon seeing another being smile, however whether that self-happiness translates to true "care" for the other being is not as obvious. In comparison, at least my own empathetic concern for the pain of others does seem more genuine. I draw this conclusion from considering the case of a purely theoretical island population, where imaginary people severely suffer. Even without directly observing their suffering, if I abstractly believed such suffering were happening, I would find myself impulsively inclined to want to reduce that suffering. Contrastingly, were these islanders to experience zero suffering at all, and a mild level of pleasure, I would be mostly indifferent as to whether they experienced even greater pleasure than they already did. (Note that the potential non-orthogonality of pleasure and pain will be discussed later in this work).

As we discussed with Rows A-C, in theory it ought to be possible to disabuse myself of this innate predisposition to feel empathy. As with racism it may not be neurally exhaustive, in that I may still possess a physical reflex to wince in the presence of say a dog being run over by a truck, however I could choose to cognitively "not care" and go about my day after witnessing such an event. If I were to deliberately strip away my empathetic impulses, the most natural result would be pure selfishness. A person who embraced pure selfishness would likely endorse (if silently, for selfish reputational reasons) concepts like slavery, child labor, torture, or consider clever approaches to murdering their own parents to access ther inheritance if applicable [19].

A complex calculus would take place behind every decision in a purely selfish mentality. Each decision that might harm others but benefit oneself would require a calculation as to whether that decision might become known, and harm one's reputation or land them under penalty by advocates for those harmed. At a societal level, it would seem most likely that any group that could emerge and maintain a majority of power (for example, a majority of control of weapons), would enter into a conspiracy to oppress the remaining population and enslave them for the purposes of maximizing productivity or other exploits of human enslavement, as was profitable in the United States [20].

It could be argued that there are at least two platforms upon which a societal decision-making framework could be built. One that abandons empathy and presumes all humans act in selfish interest alone. And another that presumes a level of human empathy where we are concerned not just with their own pain and pleasure, but with the indirect pain (and possibly pleasure) we experience vicariously and empathetically via others' pain (and possibly pleasure). It could be further argued that the degree of empathy an individual agent experiences for another being can be a continuum rather than a binary value of existing vs not. And the degree of empathy an agent espouses toward a given situation may vary not just across individual observers, but over time, classes of situations, and the target beings with whom the agent is empathizing.

We also note that the lack of empathy might not always produce pure selfishness in its simplest sense. Examples among animals, including humans, of parents' being willing to sacrifice their own direct survival needs for those of their offspring, might be attributable to selfish *gene propagation* desire as opposed to a mirroring of emotion. And that phenomenon of individual-selflessness combined with gene-propagatory selfishness, may or may not repurpose the empathic neural networks, and perhaps even in such a way that their distinction is near-impossible to disentangle. (At the time of this writing that much detail about the neural basis for empathy is not commonly known, though intuitively, certain brain areas like the right temporoparietal junction involved in theory of mind reasoning may be involved) [21]. At least theoretically, given what we know of neurology today, it is conceivable that this "gene-selfish yet self-selfless" behavior could potentially continue even among those who abandon empathy.

Despite the variance in individuals' levels of empathy towards identical situations, my own introspection will suggest (by virtue of the argument I made earlier about the general levels of similarities between human brains) that this variance is likely not so high as to render any decision-making frameworks that presuppose certain empathy levels among all humans completely useless. Provided the empathy distribution is no wider than other distributions of human psychological and biological traits (like lifespan, number of toes, and age at which language skills develop), a group of humans could develop a social system that assumes a certain parameterized and averaged level of empathy across humans and perhaps accommodates confidence intervals around that average.

A question I asked myself: why do I not de-program my own empathy such that my decisions are not biased by this layer of psychology, given that maintaining empathy reduces what would otherwise be a heuristically simple model of societal decision-making focused on my own selfish survival and gene replication drivers (often referred to as "ethical egoism")? In answering this question, one line of argument goes as follows:

1) At least a portion of my empathy exists towards other humans in my society, and "faking" this empathy rather than really feeling it would lead to imperfect mimicry that could be picked up by others, and consequently lead to their evaluation of me as overly selfish, and cause them to distrust me more than others, which could lead to suboptimal outcomes for me. For example, were I to abandon empathy, I might forget to help a blind person looking for directions at a bus stop, and that blind person might then say negative things about me out loud which could be heard by others nearby, leading to my public disfavor in that moment. For that reason, it is in my own selfish interest to maintain and cultivate my natural predisposition toward empathy rather than reject and abandon it, at least in regards to others in my society.

2) However as a heuristic, it is easier to generally embrace my disposition toward empathy, directed at a logically definable subset of entities, rather than to selectively apply it only to people in my society, because the neural complexes related to empathy (for example mirror neurons) are optimized to be generic. In other words, it is easier to care for others generally than it is to not care about an injured dog while caring about a nearby blind person. The calculations required to define a logical subset of entities that would cover all beings toward whom being empathetic would benefit my social popularity while excluding all those toward whom being empathetic would not benefit my popularity, would overwhelm my cognitive abilities. The benefit of having a logical premise that underlies this heuristic of where to apply empathy is that it allows for a simple calculation to be deployed when deciding whether to feel empathetic toward an entity so as to reduce my cognitive load.

a) For example, I could choose to declare that I am only empathetic toward people of my own skin color, and not toward any other beings. However, were I to act in accordance with this declaration, and the hypothetical blind person above were of a different skin color, my social popularity would still be negatively affected by my dismissal of their requests for help.
b) Overall, the simplest heuristic seems to be to simply extend empathy to all beings who could be empathized with. This heuristic excludes the extension of empathy to inanimate objects like stones, because everything known today about the nature of consciousness, pain and pleasure, suggests that inanimate objects do not feel pain or pleasure. Because we (humans) do feel pain and pleasure consciously, and because stones most likely do not, it is impossible to empathize with stones (as we do not know what they "feel" given we believe they feel nothing), and thus the extension of empathy must end at the juncture of sentient and non-sentient beings if we define empathy as mirroring sentiments of pain and pleasure.
c) By subscribing to a simplistic model of empathy, I can drastically reduce the cognitive load required to interpret every single social situation and explicitly decide whether to embrace my predisposition toward empathizing with another individual. This cognitive load would not just be a tax on my mental resources, but could also introduce latency in crucial situations. For example, in expressing micro-reactions to the emotional expressions of others and acting quickly in situations where empathy would help me optimize the selfish outcomes of my social interactions. The selfish likeability benefit of low-latency, reflexiveness in empathetic reactions and the reduced cognitive resource consumption of simply adopting an "identity" of being an empathetic person that I myself believe and subscribe to, seems to outweigh the costs intuitively, though that is admittedly a personal calculation I have made.

In truth, I don't believe that the above argument entirely describes my own origin of empathy. I suspect to a degree it is either innate (genetically) or so culturally inscribed within me that I cannot dispel it. I believe that even in a life devoid of any other human observers, I would display empathy toward other beings. To this degree I may have a bias toward the conclusion above against abandoning empathy.

But despite my potential bias, I suspect that the need for social popularity among people would lead most humans to feel a relatively similar degree of empathy as myself, for the selfish logical reasons described above. Moreover, it is possible that other humans have the same bias toward empathy for sentient beings as I do, and that much like the will to self-survival, the bias may be too deeply rooted in our neural apparatus to abandon. Whether or not it is so innate, this work will assume it is omnipresent and relatively tightly distributed in magnitude across people.

For flexibility, this work will use variables for the value of each person's empathy toward given situations, so that even if proposed decision-making formulae depend on proxy averages of observer-specific empathy levels, alternative proposals could build more sophisticated formulae that better deconstruct these observer-specific levels. In fact, an alternative work could build a decision-making framework modeled on an empathy level of 0 across all humans. Or evolve hierarchically parameterized frameworks wherein individuals forming a society together could input values that bias the weight of empathy in the framework up or down.

Variable Definitions

Pleasure and Pain

This work will use pleasure and pain as proxies for the fundamental emotional drivers behind all decision making. The neurotransmitters involved in pain and pleasure, such as norepinephrine, serotonin, capsaicin, dopamine, GABA and oxytocin, are obviously multi-fold and have complex interactions with each other [22, 23]. The universe of human emotions is multi-faceted and it could well be argued that simple binary concepts like pain and pleasure do not nearly capture the diversity of decision-influencing emotions.

Yet this simple reduction provides us with an initial framework upon which more complex proposals may iterate, as the many nuances behind emotional drivers become better known to humans. Additionally, there is a certain binarism implicit in most social decisions, wherein a certain behavior shall be encouraged or discouraged, and much in the way that binary computation systems underlie digital technology, the ability to reduce all decisions to a combination of binary inputs should prove highly functional, even if not perfect. Introspectively, I also notice that I am capable of feeling both pleasure and pain, and also that every other emotion I feel (love, jealousy, boredom) seems to be cognitively reducible to the impulses of pleasure and/or pain. While this work is open to alternative proposals that incorporate more sophisticated models of human drivers, because none are intuitively apparent at this time (i.e. both separate from and not reducible to, pleasure and/or pain), the Upsilon Factor formulation will use pleasure and pain as core variables.

This work is hardly alone in reducing human drives to these two variables. In general many human systems are predicated on a binary set of drivers -- e.g. "incentives and disincentives" -- which are essentially derivatives of pleasure and pain. Jeremy Bentham famously relied on these two variables for his original work on the Felicific Calculus [24].

This work will not go into the sub-components of measuring pleasure and pain, but rather leave that to other thinkers. As a placeholder model for measuring pleasure and pain, the reader could choose to use JB's Felicific Calculus as a basis, incorporating the determinants of Hedons and Dolors (e.g. propinquity, duration, etc) as means of estimating pleasure and pain. While the exact details of their measurement is beyond the scope of this text, it is unlikely to affect the primary theses of this work, which operate at the level of measured pleasure and pain with relative agnosticism to the method of measurement. It should be noted that this work does not build upon all of Jeremy Bentham's conclusions. Namely, as will be seen, it does not recommend The Greatest Happiness Principle as the variable to optimize for in societal decision-making, and there are a few other unproven assumptions and dogmatic beliefs in JB's work that do not congrue with this work. (Further discussion of differences between this work and JB's may be addressed separately.)

For simplicity in equation modeling, we will substitute Pleasure with "Joy", and Pain with "Suffering", such that we have distinct single-initial variables, J and S, to reflect Joy and Suffering respectively. These word changes are not meant to imply any semantic differentiation from "pain" and "pleasure" as commonly understood by most philosophers, economists, and psychologists.

A few definitions:

- **Target** = A sentient being experiencing joy or suffering
- **Observer** = A person, namely a decision-maker in a given social decision-making context, who is able to observe or otherwise be aware of the joy or suffering a Target experiences.
- J_i = The amount of Joy felt by an individual target being, i. (Likewise, S_i for i's suffering).
- J_{Total} = The sum amount of Joy across all sentient beings i in the universe (similarly S_{Total})
- Y = "the Upsilon Factor". Y is a function of J and S that we will define later in this work.

Direct vs Indirect Experience

An important caveat in our definition of variables J_i and S_i, is that they will include only the "direct" experiences of pleasure and pain felt by target i.

For example, take a hypothetical universe of only 10 people, numbered 1-10, where Person #8 has a coconut fall on their head, and experiences a temporary pain level of 7. Even if Person #2 observes this coconut fall and winces in vicarious pain, S_2 will be 0, while S_8 is 7.

We will endeavor to quantify the *empathetic* pain that #2 feels by observing #8, as an exogenous variable that is *separate* from S_2 or S_8. We call this variable an "Empathetic Transform" and denote it as $E_2(S_8)$. Essentially, Person #2 (as they wince while observing the coconut fall on #8's head) experiences an *empathy-weighted dilution* of S_8 (the pain felt by #8 as the coconut hits their head). The E_2 transform is usually a fractional multiplier, rendering $E_2(S_8) \leq S_8$.

The subscript "2" after the "E" refers to the fact that Person #2 might have a different empathy weighting toward Person #8's suffering than does say, Person #3, who might also have observed the coconut attack and have therefore experienced $E_3(S_8)$.

Secondary Empathetic Suffering

Person #2 might also have secondary empathetic suffering by virtue of witnessing Person #3's empathetic suffering towards Person #8. This secondary effect would be written as, for example, $E_2(E_3(S_8))$. However, the reader might notice that this "secondary empathetic factor" is usually left out of various equations in this text as the derivatives would otherwise continue ad infinitum (consider #3's observation of #2's observation of #3's observation of #8's suffering) and much like a harmonic series, these derivatives are usually too small to alter the final outputs of proposed decision functions. We can in most cases make the simplifying assumption that secondary empathetic suffering is quantitatively insignificant.

Self-Empathy

When it comes to self-empathy, we can simplify and combine the expression of empathy for an observer's self, by noting that $E_8(S_8) = S_8$. In other words, an observer (introspectively) does not feel an additional vicarious suffering for themselves over and above their direct suffering as a target. (I posit that self-pity can simply be considered a form of direct suffering, and it is not quite the same as actually observing one's own suffering, but is more of a process of rationalizing about one's suffering).

Summations of Empathetic Suffering

The total direct suffering in this universe ignores $E(S_i)$ for all individuals i from 1 to 10. Thus $S_{Total} = Sum(S_1, S_2...S_{10})$. Let's assume that S_{10} is actually yourself: the reader. In this case, your empathy-weighted suffering is your direct suffering (in your existence as a target) plus your empathetic concern for the other 9 individuals' suffering (in your existence as an observer), the sum of both being written as:

$S_{10}+E_{10}(S_1)+E_{10}(S_2)...+E_{10}(S_9)$

Since $S_{10}=E_{10}(S_{10})$, it might be tempting to combine all the terms to be written as $E_{10}(S_1+S_2...+S_{10})$, or $E_{10}(S_{Total})$. This simplification is not a perfect mathematical operation however. For example, if Person #8 in the coconut example experienced 7 units of suffering from the coconut, and Person #4 also had an object fall on them (but it was only an acorn) and suffered 3 units, then the combined suffering is 10 units. However, empathetic suffering evaluations are not transitive among targets. In other words, it would not be true to say that the reader's empathetic concern for this combination of pain is equivalent to the empathetic concern the reader might have of any situation leading to 10 total units of suffering (e.g. if Person #8 had simply experienced 10 units of suffering themselves and Person #4 experienced none). This discrepancy results because a given observer may empathize more with Person #4 than Person #8 or vice versa. In a similar vein, the reader may have previously had a coconut accident that sensitizes them to have disproportionately greater empathetic concern for coconut-caused suffering than acorn-caused suffering.

In order to avoid propagating the concept that every victim of suffering is equally empathized with (be it a squid believed to be sentient or oneself), we will introduce the variable EWS ("empathy-weighted suffering") and where there is no subscript the empathetic vantage point will always be assumed to be the reader acting as an observer, i.e. $EWS = E_{Reader}WS$. EWS_{Total} is the total empathetic concern for suffering the reader has to all individuals suffering in the universe, which in the fictional universe above would be equivalent to $E_{10}(S_1)+E_{10}(S_2)...+E_{10}(S_{10})$. Likewise, EWS_i will be the empathetic concern the reader has for the suffering of individual i, or equivalently $E_{10}(S_i)$. Because the "reader" is meant to represent any individual in a social decision-making system who might be party to said decision-making system, we can use $E_{Reader}WS$ and $E_{Observer}WS$ interchangeably.

Additional Empathy-Weighting Caveats

Empathy-Weighted Joy

We could introduce an equivalent empathy-weighted joy (EWJ) concept, though this work likely will not make much of it due to the unclear empathy that's felt for the joy others experience. Regardless, J_i and J_{Total} still correspond to the direct joy that an individual or the sum of all individuals in a universe, respectively, experience.

Parameterizing Empathetic Weighting

EWS, may also be time dependent, as it may be sensitive to the mood of the observer. This variability can be modeled by separating $E_{T1,Observer}WS$ from $E_{T2,Observer}WS$ for timestamps T1 and T2 respectively, or as $E_{T\text{-Avg, Observer}}WS$ for the average $E_{Observer}WS$ over all time.

There may be other dimensions of the observation to factor into EWS as well, though for the purposes of this work, we will not delve into this variability much and mostly focus on the average empathy-weighting an individual observer might have for any given sentient beings. In general, any additional parameters under consideration will be notated as comma-delimited subscripts to the variable being parameterized.

How Orthogonal Are Joy and Suffering?

Jeremy Bentham essentially equated Pain and Pleasure on a single spectrum such that they could be added and subtracted from one another to derive a single variable he called "happiness": equal to Pleasure minus Pain.

An opposite extreme would be to say that Pain and Pleasure are completely orthogonal, and that there is no situation in which the addition of Pleasure can act as a dampener of Pain or vice versa within a target consciousness.

At the time of this writing, I have an imperfect and vague introspective understanding of their interaction, and believe it is neither of the two extremes: neither are Pain and Pleasure perfectly interchangeable nor are they perfectly unrelated.

I will posit that pain and pleasure are, at their core, independent and unique phenomena that a consciousness can experience. They could be thought of as represented by different neurological synaptic pathways that can be activated or deactivated by various neurotransmitters. It might be that the exact behavior of neurotransmitters in the brain at any given time can "tip" a consciousness toward activating one neural pathway (say pain), more than another (say pleasure), or perhaps stimulate both simultaneously. It might also be that when the circumstances are ripe for both neural pathways to be activated, the "volume" of one pathway (i.e. the attention paid to the experience of pain or pleasure) may be attenuated by the distraction that the other causes. Essentially, if a person is experiencing pain, it might be that a dose of pleasure *distracts* that person from the pain, thus lessening the overall experience of the pain, even if the causal agent of the pain subsists.

To take a concrete example, let's imagine a person, Frank, who simultaneously has an achy back and is consuming a cone of ice cream. If Frank has an ache on the left side of his back while walking to the ice cream store to purchase the ice cream, he might experience an S_{Frank} of say, 1.5 units due to his ache, and a J_{Frank} of 0.7 units during his walk (let's assume the weather is nice and there are friendly and familiar faces at the ice cream store). So Frank may be experiencing an underlying minimum pain of 1.0, but his attention vacillates between the suffering and the joy. S_{Frank} might get stimulated up to 2.5 when Frank happens to shift slightly more weight to his left side, and conversely the joy of his environment might be able to partially distract him from the pain, but never enough to decrease S_{Frank} below 1.0 at any time. On average, between the "distracted pain", the "intensified pain", and the "undistracted pain" levels, it might be the case that the time-weighted average of S_{Frank} is 1.5 during his walk.

Once Frank starts eating the ice cream, his J_{Frank} might increase from 0.7 to 3.0 as dopamine and other neurotransmitters react to the sugar and saturated fat. This sudden increase in Joy may also distract Frank's attention enough from the back ache, that is average S_{Frank} of 1.5 actually drops to an average of 1.2, especially immediately after a bite is taken and his system is largely overwhelmed by the influx of carbohydrates. In this way, J_{Frank} actually changes S_{Frank}.

This non-orthogonality makes the precise definition of a calculus for decision-making based on J and S rather complex. The 0.3 reduction in S_{Frank} could be considered to "come from" the 2.3 increase in J_{Frank}, and accordingly it might be argued that was actually a 2.6 unit increase in J_{Frank} but that 0.3 was transferred to S_{Frank} reduction. However, the level of assumption needed to make that kind of statement is beyond what can be proven or very logically deduced based on current scientific fact or even introspection. Regardless, the 0.3 reduction in S_{Frank} is in fact a reduction, even if the cause of the reduction was the distraction due to the new J_{Frank} that captured Frank's conscious attention. We can use the variable $S_{Distraction}$ to specifically count these Joy-induced Suffering Reductions, and given the quantities negative valence since they reduce S, rendering the $S_{Distraction}$ of Frank eating ice cream to be -0.3.

A Note On Derivational Approach

As mentioned earlier, this work draws largely from introspection, and from the general belief that most humans have similar neural systems, and thus that these introspections will enjoy universal resonance. These introspections examine intuitive empathetic responses to various scenarios that echo sacrificial dilemmas and common trolley problems.

In deriving the upsilon function, I started with a series of simple optimization functions and tested them against such sacrificial dilemmas. For example, take Jeremy Bentham's "Greatest Happiness Principle" (GHP), which could be modeled as $\max(H)$ where $H = J_{Total} - S_{Total}$. Aside from failing to take into account empathy-weighting (JB might argue that each individual observer's EWs all cancel each other out, and that for non-human beings, the actual sentient experience of suffering is lower than humans in accordance with how we'd intuitively value their pain; whereas I believe that even in cases where non-humans do experience the same level of pain as human, most of us would simply find it difficult to empathize with their pain to the same degree as they could their own personal pain or that of any other human), his potential equatation of Joy and Suffering fails an intuitive sacrificial dilemma i'll call "First Islands".

Scenario 1: First Islands

<u>The Base Case</u>
Imagine the *First Islands Universe* contains only one island, called Blue Island.

On Blue Island, 50 people live for 100 years in a pure state of suffering then instantly vanish. S_{Total} of Blue Island (S_{Blue} for short) is 5000 units, where each person-year of suffering is worth 1 S unit for this scenario.

Since the Universe is only composed of Blue island, $S_{Blue} = S_{Total} = 5000$, $J_{Total} = 0$, and in the Greatest Happiness Principle, we define H to equal Happiness, which is $J_{Total}-S_{Total}$, we end up with H = -5000.

<u>The Abundance Option</u>
Imagine you have the opportunity to snap your fingers, and alter the Base Case such that a separate and totally isolated island, Green Island, suddenly appears in the *First Islands Universe* for the same 100 year span.

On Green Island, 1 million people live in pure unadulterated glee for 100 years then instantly vanish painlessly. J_{Total} of Green Island (J_{Green} for short) is 100 million units, where each person-year of glee is worth 1 Joy unit for this scenario.

Since the *Universe*'s population is now the sum of Blue and Green's population, the total H = J-S = 99,995,000 units, which is much more promising from a GHP standpoint.

<u>The Minimalist Option</u>
Let's say as an alternative to the Abundance Option, you have the option to alter the Base Case such that life on Blue Island never existed. If you take this option, the First Islands Universe contains $J_{Total} = 0$, and $S_{Total} = 0$, as there's only one island and no life exists on it. As such, H = $J_{Total}-S_{Total}$ = 0.

The Happiness levels for each case in the First Islands scenario are as follow:
- Base Case, H = -5,000
- Abundance Case, H = almost 100 million, and
- Minimalist Case, H = 0

The Greatest Happiness Principle would suggest we should max(H) and therefore clearly choose the Abundance Case, even though the residents of Blue Island suffer unabated.

Essentially, the GHP suggests that if we have a population of suffering people, rather than try to solve their suffering, we would (were the choice mutually exclusive) spawn a large number of happy people elsewhere who can "make up" for the suffering of the 10 originals. By extension, the solution to poverty and pain on Earth might then be to simply birth a plethora of happy babies, and the total number of happy people will blind us to the suffering of the few. In fact, to make this argument even more absurd, assuming the joy of rats is empathetically low but not zero, by GHP there should be a number (less than infinity) of new rats that could be introduced into the universe to justify all the current pain and suffering of humans provided the rats were net more joyous than suffered.

However, introspectively the minimalist case is much more preferable. If given the opportunity to end the suffering of a small population, with no change to the rest of the Universe, it would resonate more with instinctual empathetic impulses to terminate this suffering than to attempt to "blind ourselves" to the suffering by simply spawning additional beings who experience pleasure. No amount of pleasure in a separate being seems to empathetically "neutralize" or erase the pain of a given consciousness. Thus, abiding by the GHP, letting Upsilon (Y) = H, and striving for $\max(H)=J_{Total}-S_{Total}$, fails our introspective empathy tests as a definition for the Upsilon Factor.

Continuing through iterations of similar exercises, it becomes apparent that there is no one-line formula that intuitively captures the entire empathetic impulse. Instead, there is a *function* composed of a hierarchical "echelon" of *factors*, which empathy drives us to optimize in order.

Rather than stepping through each iteration, this work will summarize the proposed function and the sub-component factors, of which Upsilon is only one (but a key one), in their hierarchical order. Separate works may cover the various iterations that were trialed against sacrificial dilemmas and other similar thought experiments and scenarios.

The Snowball

The broader function that houses the Upsilon Factor is called "The Snowball" in this work. It contains 4 factors.

Omega: The Threshold of Intolerable Suffering

Omega is a value of EWS_{Total} for a given universe, that represents the absolute maximum amount of empathic suffering an individual can accept in order to voluntarily continue their own survival.

Using a simple universe of 10 people (i = 1 to 10), with the observer as person #10, we can consider Omega from the standpoint of the observer (or reader) as:

$$\text{Omega must be} > E_{10}(S_1)+E_{10}(S_2)...+E_{10}(S_{10})$$
$$\text{or}$$
$$\text{Omega must be} > E_{10}WS_{Total}$$

This factor definition can be read as "Omega must be greater than my empathetic perception of the total suffering in the Universe."

As long as Person #10's direct suffering, $S_{10}=E(S_{10})$, plus their empathy-weighted suffering on account of the suffering of Persons #1-9, all add up to less than Omega, Person #10 would choose to continue surviving.

Any agency Person 10 had over the Universe to alter it such that EWS_{Total} could be brought below Omega, would take precedence over any other action or decision Person #10 could take, because the only alternative to bringing EWS below Omega would be to seek self-termination.

A couple pragmatic examples of this would be a situation where the observer (Person #10) themselves were experiencing unbearable pain and torture to the point where they wished death upon themselves, and/or, a situation where Person #10 were given a choice to stop Person #9 from being tortured in front of them in exchange for painless self-termination. In such a situation, no other factors besides the cessation of this intolerable pain could take precedence to Person #10, introspectively.

In summary, the Omega Factor is:

$$E_iWS_{Total} \text{ must be} < Omega, \text{ for any societal decision maker, i.}$$

We maximize the ratio of consensus-buildability to dogmatic presumption by prioritizing the Omega Factor above any other decision making criteria in a human-run society.

Alpha: The Maintenance Of Will To Survive

Once a person has deemed that a given choice among a set of options will not betray the Omega factor, the criterion prioritized next for evaluating social decisions is for an observer to accomplish enough personal Joy to warrant a basic will to survive.

Without any will to survive at all, survival would end. For example, a person might allow themselves to languish, accrue infections, exert very little effort into healthy eating and fitness, experience emotional depression, and eventually die early.

For this reason, humans strive for J_{Self} to be greater than a threshold Alpha, essentially as a survival mechanism. This basic Alpha level of Joy does not require much in the way of resources. For example, people derive a non-zero amount of Joy from simply breathing, or drinking water after a period of thirst. But if Alpha were not satisfied, it is unlikely that a person would prioritize any other issue, unless it threatened the Omega Factor.

Note that Alpha is centered only on self Joy, and not on the Joy of others. While the Suffering of others can cause a person to be willing to sacrifice their own Joy, the Joy of others is introspectively never more important than our own basic Joy necessary to continue choosing to survive.

We formally write out the Alpha factor as:

$$J_{Self} \text{ must be } > Alpha$$

Upsilon: The Reduction of Empathy-Weighted Suffering

From Binary to Gradated; Hierarchical to Interactive

Before defining the Upsilon Factor, it's worth acknowledging that the latter two factors of the Snowball, Upsilon and Zeta, are not as cleanly hierarchical as Omega and Alpha are as decision-making criteria.

Omega and Alpha are, practically, binary considerations. Any given decision a person confronts can be evaluated based on whether any options for that decision would violate the thresholds Omega or Alpha. However, Upsilon and Zeta, as will be detailed, are minimization and maximization functions (respectively), thus are in theory "infinitely optimizable". This infiniteness implies that in the case of a strict hierarchy, no human would ever focus their attention on Zeta. Because even the act of spending time and attention on Zeta could be modeled as a decision to not spend that time and attention on Upsilon.

An overly simplistic way to consider the priority between Upsilon and Zeta would be to think of them in the context of any decision that could significantly impact either and where that impact could be measurable or "visible" to the decider. In such a case, when it is easy to see that a given decision could affect Upsilon negatively, I will propose that our empathetic predisposition would be to decide in favor of improving Upsilon, even if it entailed harming Zeta. A more full and sophisticated treatment of the interaction effects between Upsilon and Zeta will follow their definitions.

Upsilon Definition

Subject to Omega and Alpha, the next priority for a person is the Upsilon Factor, which aims to minimize empathetic suffering. While the Omega Factor captures the portion of EWS minimization that suffices to save a person from self-termination, Upsilon is a person's desire to further reduce empathetic pain.

Upsilon is defined as:

$$min(Y), \text{ where } Y = (EWS_{Total})$$

As we noted in our earlier definition of EWS, from the standpoint of an observer, EWS stands for the total suffering across all sentient beings in the Universe, as a weighted sum with each being's suffering weighted by an empathy-weighting unique to the observer. Importantly, this includes the observer's *own* suffering (where the empathy-weighting is expected to be the highest among all target beings). In fact, it is likely the case that the majority of daily decisions made with respect to Upsilon by a typical person are dominated by their effect on S_{Self}, and that S_{Self} (equal to EWS_{Self}) is the single largest addend in the sum of EWS_{Total} for any given observer.

The reasoning behind why the title of this work highlights Upsilon more than the other factors will be discussed in a dedicated section.

Importantly, we'll note that the reduction of suffering takes precedence over any creation of Joy beyond the Alpha threshold. This principle addresses the conundrum raised by the "First Islands" scenario described earlier, wherein intuition would suggest we prioritize reducing the pain on Blue Island over creating new joy on Green Island. Upsilon also intuitively aligns with my intuitive response to a series of other sacrificial dilemmas.

The crucial thesis here is that when hard-pushed to make a decision that could lead to increased or reduced suffering among ourselves or others, our empathetic impulses tend to lead us to prioritize reducing suffering over increasing joy. While there are exceptions, as will be discussed in the "Upsilon and Zeta" trade-offs section, a mnemonic example would be to consider whether you would take a winning lottery ticket that could change your life fortune if you knew that doing so would lead to the painful death of an innocent stranger. The only way a person would take the ticket, assuming no other complicating factors were involved, would be by suspending their empathetic impulses (as discussed earlier in the "Empathy" section).

Zeta: The Pursuit of Joy

Following from the logic set forth in the Upsilon definition, Zeta is the lowest priority component of the Snowball Function. Subject to a set of choices where Omega and Alpha are satisfied, and Upsilon is not knowingly and predictably affected, our inclination will be to maximize our own Joy.

Zeta is thus defined as:

$$Max(Zeta), where\ Zeta = J_{Self}$$

Similar to the way in which Upsilon "builds" on Omega by extending a person's investment in reducing EWS beyond the Omega threshold, Zeta builds upon Alpha by extending a person's investment in increasing their own Joy beyond the Alpha threshold.

However, as discussed earlier, Zeta does not optimize for the "empathy-weighted Joy" of others. An alternative version of the Snowball could replace J in both Alpha and Zeta with EWJ, and in fact such an alternate version would congrue perfectly with the rest of this work. Essentially this work puts forth the hypothesis that the only addend in EWJ that has a non-zero value is J_{Self}.

This controversial agnosticism toward empathetic Joy is certainly debatable. But introspectively, I find that even when I try to help loved ones get the most out of their lives, it is motivated by a desire to reduce their suffering as opposed to a desire to increase their Joy. A caveat is that as noted in the earlier variable definition section, the non-orthogonality of Joy and Suffering imply that there is an $S_{Distraction}$ value of events that increase J_{Others}, that would influence the Upsilon factor for an observer, and may motivate a person's desire to bring joy to other people: rather to reduce others' suffering by way of distraction, than specifically to maximize others' joy for its own end. Because any such changes would be "double counted" in both the EWS_{Total} and a theoretical EWJ_{Total}, it suffices to tabulate only the EWS_{Total} value and replace EWJ_{Total} with J_{Self}.

Summarizing All Four Factors

The following chart summarizes all four factors of the Snowball Function.

Table 2: Snowball Function Factors

Factor	Intuition	Equation	Priority
Omega	At all costs, we wish to maintain empathetic global suffering below an intolerable level	Keep EWS_{Total} < Omega	1
Alpha	Subject to Omega, we wish to maintain the will to survive	Keep J_{Self} > Alpha	2
Upsilon	Subject to Alpha, we wish to minimize our empathetic perception of total global suffering	Minimize $Y = EWS_{Total}$	3
Zeta	Subject to visible conflicts with Upsilon, we wish to maximize our personal Joy	Maximize Zeta = J_{Self}	4

The fundamental thesis of this work is that by collectively following the hierarchy laid out in the above Snowball Function, humans can maximize consensus in social decisions while minimizing their reliance on axiomatic and unprovable assumptions, i.e. in the most objective manner possible.

Trading Off Upsilon and Zeta

As mentioned earlier, the hierarchy between Zeta and Upsilon is not entirely strict. If it were, then practically every waking moment of a person's life, where Omega and Alpha are typically satisfied, would be spent exclusively focused on Upsilon as opposed to self-joy. Yet, we as humans likely spend a great deal of our time focused on Zeta.

In defense of the Snowball hierarchy, it may be the case that much of the time one might initially consider to be an expense invested in Zeta fulfillment, is actually a focus on $S_{Distraction}$ reduction. In other words, we focus on how to avoid future suffering for ourselves by using joy as a distraction.

But it would be intuitively inaccurate to suggest that humans are never predispositioned to pursue their own joy beyond the modicum needed to distract themselves from suffering. What is more likely, is that when confronting multiple options for a significant decision, X, where the consequences of $X_{Option1}$, $X_{Option2}$, etc, are intuited by the decision-maker to have an effect of EWS_{Total}, the option which reduces EWS_{Total} is chosen over any other option, even one that raises J_{Self}. In that sense, the strictness of the hierarchy between Upsilon and Zeta may likely be proportional to the importance of the decision at hand.

We'll examine a few examples next. While this work is focused on the application of the Snowball to social decision-making, the first few examples that examine the Upsilon vs Zeta trade-offs will begin with single individual decision-making scenarios, to understand the "microeconomics" of the trade-offs.

Scenario 2: Joy Drug

Universe and Options

Let's say Bob has an opportunity on a Sunday afternoon to ingest a psychedelic drug with absolutely no disruptive side effects.

This drug simply raises J_{Bob} by 5 units by delivering Bob 4 hours of euphoria.

In theory, Bob could spend that same 4 hours cleaning up the living quarters of a homeless person, Clark, on the street outside his home, instead of taking this euphoric drug. Clark is experiencing suffering greater than 5 units (the exact number will not affect this calculation).

Let's say that this 4 hours of cleanup would reduce S_{Clark} by 5 units, and E_{Bob} for S_{Clark} is 2%. Thus the reduction in $E_{Bob}(S_{Clark})$ of taking this time to clean up is 0.1 units (2% of 5 units). Said differently, $E_{Bob}(S_{Clark,Clean}) = -0.1$.

However, EWS_{Total} also has an $E_{Bob}(S_{Bob})$ factor.

Since Bob would be knowingly forfeiting the opportunity for 5 units of J_{Bob} during the 4 hours he was cleaning, and might not enjoy the work involved of cleaning, the S_{Bob} of cleaning while envying the alternative option would be non-zero. Let's assume $S_{Bob} = 0.5$ if Bob chooses to clean instead of take the drug (compared to S_{Bob} of 0 if taking the drug). Accordingly, $E_{Bob}(S_{Bob,Clean}) = 0.5$.

In this case, the total change in $E_{Bob}WS_{Total}$ would be +0.4 units of suffering ($E_{Bob}(S_{Bob,Clean})$ + $E_{Bob}(S_{Clark,Clean})$), if Bob were to clean instead of take the drug.

Decision Analysis

So in order for Bob to improve his evaluation of Upsilon by reducing $E_{Bob}WS_{Total}$ it would be optimal to not clean. (Note that $E_{Clark}WS$ doesn't weigh into the decision here because there is only one decision maker about Bob's decision: Bob).

While *not cleaning* is not the same as taking the drug, once Bob has decided not to clean, it would be purely beneficial to his computed Zeta to take the drug, and this action would have no effect on Upsilon.

So, taking the drug is compatible with the Snowball hierarchy for Bob as the sole decision maker of his actions.

What the Joy Drug scenario demonstrates is that in most situations where there is an opportunity for Zeta improvement that does not in itself threaten Upsilon, it is actually that case that not taking the Zeta improvement opportunity in fact also hurts Upsilon, because: a) the knowledge of forsaken Zeta improvement causes mild "missed opportunity" suffering we can call $S_{Missing\ Out}$, and b) the labor required to reduce others' suffering may incur self-suffering.

However, this argument could be taken to the extreme. Let's examine another example scenario:

Scenario 3: Good Samaritan
Imagine Lisa were walking to an ice cream store. She is very excited about eating ice cream, and has not had ice cream in a long time. She will reach the ice cream store in 10 minutes and receive $J_{Lisa,IceCreamConsumption}$ of 7 units once she consumes ice cream. However, for each minute she is late to commencing the consumption of ice cream, because her appetite has peaked and her mood may soon shift, $J_{Lisa,IceCreamConsumption}$ will decrease by 1 unit. On the way to the store, she sees a blind man, Todd, walking across the street who is about to trip on a fallen branch. No one else is around and Lisa could ignore Todd and it would never cause any direct suffering to Lisa. However, Todd would experience S_{Todd} of 30 units if he fell. Lisa would take 1 minute to remove the branch from Todd's way, and it would cause no discernible direct S_{Lisa} for her to do so -- the act of walking and bending down to pick up the branch is no inconvenience to her. However, she would lose 1 unit of $J_{Lisa,IceCreamConsumption}$ by not quenching her desire for ice cream at the optimal craving instant, and she is cognizant of this fact. Her empathetic coefficient E_{Lisa} for S_{Todd} is 15%. It is 10% for any given stranger, but she intuitively believes that blind people are more sensitive to suffering due to a compounding effect with other suffering they experience in their daily lives, as well as more fear of the unknown if they fall (for example being able to see how far away vehicles are), rendering her coefficient for Todd 15%. As such, if Lisa does not help Todd, $E_{Lisa}WS$ is 4.5 units (15% of 30 units) and J_{Lisa} is 7 units. If Lisa does help Todd, $E_{Lisa}WS$ is reduced to 0 units and J_{Lisa} is reduced to 6 units.

In the Good Samaritan scenario, the Snowball would suggest that helping Todd would optimize Lisa's Upsilon factor which is a higher priority than optimizing her Zeta factor by racing to the ice cream store, and therefore Lisa would help Todd.

In comparing the Good Samaritan Scenario to the Joy Drug Scenario, it's important to consider precisely how much the feeling of "missing out" on a joyful experience causes an increase in self suffering as opposed to a decrease in self joy. Missing out on a romantic or professional opportunity that would cause a person to grieve later, typically leads to an increase in S and threatens Upsilon. If the Good Samaritan scenario were altered such that Joy were late to an interview (instead of an ice cream) and missing it by 1 minute would alter her future career/life in a direly negative manner, it might not be as obvious that she would stop to help Todd (we presume the prospective employer were unlikely to believe her story, and we do not assign factual merit to the superstitiousness of Karma). Perhaps Todd's fall would be very minor, he would simply get up and keep walking, and if Lisa were truly omniscient about the trade offs, a life of career regret might not be worth the empathetic pain reduction. In reality, most people do not have this omniscience, and it is not predictable that 1 minute of tardiness would lead to job loss, nor that a given job opportunity would lead with certainty to greater Joy than an alternative job opportunity. These elements of reality are why in most cases humans would stop to help prevent a blind person's fall even if it made them late to a job interview. But this conclusion cannot be said to be absolute, and it depends on the circumstantial EWS trade-offs. Compared to trade-off situations weighing samaritanship against Joyous opportunities with scant "regret of missing out" S_{Self} tax, EWS trade-off situations that operate mostly in the realm of Upsilon optimization are much more likely to be controversial to the decider.

While it may be possible to concoct a scenario where Zeta gets prioritized over Upsilon, this work concludes based on the lack of such scenarios at hand, that as a first approximation, strictly prioritizing Upsilon over Zeta congrues with intuitive empathetic impulses.

A Deeper Examination Of Upsilon / Zeta Trade Offs

I will admit to a certain amount of unease around the ambiguity of the trade offs between Upsilon and Zeta. This work will simply acknowledge that there is more disambiguation to be done between the priorities of EWS_{Total} and J_{Self}. In effort to placate the reader's concerns and restore faith in the broader Snowball hierarchy, we'll examine a couple more example scenarios here.

Scenario 4: Volunteering Retiree

Imagine a successful entrepreneur, Tracy, has sold their company for enough money that they are confident they no longer need employment for financial survival. They retire early and resolve to enjoy life.

While they pursue inspiring art projects and consume entertainment, there happen to be volunteer opportunities available to help deliver meals to isolated senior citizens who are suffering in a town 1 hour away.

If Tracy were to spend 5 hours a day volunteering, they would reduce S_i by 2 units for each senior citizen i, and could serve roughly 15 such citizens, totaling 30 units.

Tracy might be said to have 15% empathic weight for these unfamiliar seniors, making the daily $E_{Tracy}WS_{Total}$ reduction value of volunteering 4.5 units/day.

While Tracy derives about 4 units per day of J_{Tracy} from directing those same 5 hours toward entertainment, it's not immediately obvious what the S_{Tracy} increment of volunteering instead of consuming entertainment would be as Tracy wouldn't necessarily dislike the volunteer work and might enjoy the camaraderie.

Yet, Tracy feels a sense of cognitive dissonance in devoting their day toward this volunteer work, which seems to neither optimally utilize their faculties nor provide them with the sense of "reward" they yearn for on account of having toiled for decades to successfully retire.

The volunteering scenario might on surface suggest that Tracy would, if acting in accordance with the Snowball, prioritize Upsilon over Zeta and devote 5 hours a day to volunteering. Yet we see that this decision would result in cognitive dissonance, for multiple reasons.

The first is a sense that Tracy feels they have "earned" the J_{Tracy} that ought to result from the S_{Tracy} that had been previously invested in their business. It could be argued that not receiving this expected J_{Tracy} could potentially be modeled as a form of $S_{Missing\ Out}$ (as described in the Joy Drug scenario earlier), wherein Tracy's cognitive knowledge of the fact they endured all that prior S_{Tracy} from their career of toil without getting the resultant J_{Tracy} reward causes them to feel emotional regret over their prior decisions and thus actually increases S_{Tracy}. The fact that Tracy knew they could have been enjoying themselves and expected to do so, then missed out on that expectation may trigger mental jealousy circuits that cause psychological suffering.

Scenario 5: Injected Joy Drug

Imagine a universe containing an individual, Charles, who is told about a drug similar to the Joy Drug described earlier, that provides 5 units of $J_{Charles}$ by triggering 4 hours of euphoria with no subsequent suffering of any kind.

However, in order to take the drug, Charles must receive it via a syringe injection, which will cause 1 unit of $S_{Charles}$.

In the Injected Joy Drug scenario, I propose that Charles would make the decision of whether or not to take the drug dependent on the context of the broader Suffering and Joy on his life.

For example, say Charles were curious about this drug, and had never taken it before. This curiosity might cause desire, and that desire might cause suffering when not satiated, in the form of $S_{Unrequited\ Desire}$. This notion of desire may seem unintuitive in that the satiation of desire could be considered a form of Joy. However, as many philosophers have opined in the past (See "Samudhya", [25]), introspectively the presence of desire without its satiation and without distraction from it, eventually "festers" and becomes a form of suffering. The difference between $S_{Unrequited\ Desire}$ and $S_{Missing\ Out}$ is not particularly important to delineate or perfectly distinguish, as they are similar forms of "synthetic" suffering. One way to consider the difference between them is that missing out can be in response to prior *expected joy* whereas unrequited desire operates on *anticipated and desired but not necessarily expected joy*. Once Charles learned of this opportunity, and began to build anticipation of the 5 J_{Drug} units, deciding against taking the drug purely on the basis of the fear of the 1 unit of $S_{Syringe}$ would lead to $S_{Unrequited\ Desire}$ that might be greater than 1 unit. Thus without even considering the Zeta factor, Upsilon optimization would cause Charles to take the drug. This curiosity component is interesting in that it "converts" the unrequited anticipation of what would otherwise be J into S, similar to $S_{Missing\ Out}$. Both of these synthetic suffering computations hint at a very volatile function for J wherein it can convert into S when teased to a person. Separate works may need to excavate this issue further.

However, it's not entirely clear that the only deterrent against forfeiting the opportunity is $S_{Unrequited\ Desire}$. It seems intuitively likely that given a high enough J_{Drug} opportunity (imagine it were 1000 units of Joy), $S_{Syringe}$ of 1 unit would surely be worth the cost, even if Charles had taken the drug before and thus the curiosity component were not relevant. It is also likely the case that the anticipation of the 1000 $J_{Charles}$ units brings about a form of $S_{Distraction}$ suffering mitigation that could exceed the -1 $S_{Charles}$ units needed to "unblock" Zeta pursuit within the Snowball framework.

Nuance of Distractibility

The Injected Joy Drug case opens an intricate issue around synthetic suffering offsets like $S_{Distraction}$, $S_{Unrequited\ Desire}$, and $S_{Missing\ Out}$, from J_{Self}. Consider the case where J_{Self} could be obtained from an act that led to S_i for a separate being, i. Could the EWS_i be offset by an $S_{Distraction}$ benefit of J_{Self}? In practice this offset would imply that a person might engage in an act for joy even knowing that this act causes another person pain.

We posit that an $S_{Distraction}$ offset could in fact cause a person to seek J_{Self} at the cost of $E_{Self}(S_{Other})$. However, $S_{Distraction}$ has a hidden subscript "self" rendering it $S_{Distraction,Self}$. In other words, $S_{Distraction}$ counts against S_{Self} but not against S_{Other} directly. So only in a situation where the J_{Self} actually led to distraction against a form of S_{Self} that was in play in a given decision, could the decision output be to accept S_{Other} in exchange for J_{Self}.

For example, if a person A could instantly receive a cone of ice cream, at the expense of another person B stubbing their toe, then A would forfeit the ice cream given no other context, in accordance with the Snowball. However, if A had climbed a mountain and A's legs were in pain, and this ice cream would help distract A from the pain, then A might opt for the ice cream, even at the expense of B's pain.

This nuance of distractibility is quite impactful, as it renders critical the degree to which self-joy gets converted to the mitigation of self-suffering, not just to decisions involving self-suffering exclusively, but to decisions that may involve the empathy-weighted suffering of others as well.

The perceived violation of this principle is at the heart of many societal concerns that the public often gripes about. Commonly, people in leadership positions are capable of becoming so addicted to J_{Self} that they do in fact accept S_{Other} for their own selfish gain. Three manners in which this phenomenon can emerge are:

1. **Low Empathy Coefficients**. Certain leaders, typically called "sociopaths", may in fact have statistically lower empathy coefficients for S_{Others}.
2. **Withdrawal**. Certain leaders may initially not be aware that the actions they are taking lead to S_{Others}, and the financial (or other) gain from these actions leads to a standard of living, that would make disruption cause them S_{Self} were the actions to no longer be taken. As such, the comparative influence of S_{Others} on EWS_{Total} is diluted by the potential effect on S_{Self}.
3. **Dogmatism**. The moral centers of the brain may latch onto beliefs in dogmatic, deontological principles, and convince the leaders that there is a "higher purpose" beyond the suffering and joy of sentient beings. In this case, it is not strictly J_{Self} that trumps the leader's Upsilon Factor concerns, but an entirely orthogonal value system to the Snowball.

This work aims to convince the reader that resolute focus on the Snowball hierarchy of factors, leads not only to consistent social consensus buildability, but also to internal logical consistency with observable fact. A strict observance of logic and facts will lead to less cognitive dissonance internally, and because our neurology is hard-coded, the Snowball hierarchy will withstand and outlast momentary distortions like dogmatism and withdrawal effects as a framework for making decisions.

Why The Focus on Upsilon?

At this juncture, the reader may wonder why the title of this book highlights Upsilon as opposed to the entire Snowball.

The earlier section describing trade offs between Upsilon and Zeta demonstrated that where there is controversy between the two, Upsilon will take precedence. Additionally, Omega and Alpha are largely "taken care of" for most people who are alive (as otherwise they might have pursued suicide). As a result, the vast majority of decisions people make that might affect others, are with respect to Upsilon.

As this work primarily seeks to develop a template for social decision-making, factors within the Snowball that are mostly focused on the self (Omega, Alpha and Zeta) can largely be left out of consideration when it comes to the application of this template. The arena where social decisions such as governmental policy and legislations come into play, are almost entirely dictated by trade offs between the suffering of one party versus another.

For that reason, the main takeaway from this work is the importance of the Upsilon Factor, min(EWS). Many of the examples of the application of Upsilon so far have focused on unilateral decisions by a single decision maker. Coming up in this work, we will briefly discuss examples of how the Upsilon Factor comes into play in social decisions.

Applying the Upsilon Factor

As mentioned earlier, the application of this work to a single decision-maker focused on their own personal trade-offs is not particularly useful. The value of this work comes from its application to consensus-building between humans. This work itself will not endeavor to litigate popular policy issues based on the Upsilon Factor, but as exemplars, a few situations may help demonstrate how such litigation could proceed.

Three-Person Universe

Empathy-Weighting Matrix

Imagine a three-person universe with actors Larry, Mary, and Nancy. The universe also contains 5 crustacean crabs, who may exhibit signs of consciousness, but are not party to decision-making in the universe. We may consider each decision-maker -- Larry, Mary and Nancy -- as having a unique "baseline empathy weighting" for each other being in the Universe. This $E_{Observer}(S_{Target})$ matrix can be represented as follows:

Table 3: Empathy Weighting Matrix for Three-Person Universe

Target	Observer: E_{Larry}	Observer: E_{Mary}	Observer: E_{Nancy}
S_{Larry}	1	15%	15%
S_{Mary}	15%	1	20%
S_{Nancy}	15%	20%	1
$S_{Crab-[n]}$	5%	3%	3%

A few observations on the baseline Empathy Weighting Matrix:
1. The empathy-weightings Larry, Mary and Nancy have to their own personal suffering are always 100%, as nobody's suffering matters to them as much as their own
2. We make the assumption in this universe that generally, most of the people empathize 15% about the other humans (who we shall assume know each other since they are co-decision-makers).
3. However because Mary and Nancy are both female, we arbitrarily assume they are slightly more capable of empathizing with each other than they are with Larry or vice versa (due to shared female experiences), bringing Mary and Nancy's inter-EW to 20%.
4. Arbitrarily, we also attribute gender differences to the empathy weighting humans have with the other species in question here, crabs. We assume Larry is slightly more empathetic to the crabs (5%) than are Mary and Nancy (3%).

The biases introduced above are meant to illustrate the fact that in the real world, it is likely the case that various groups and individuals have variant empathy weightings with respect to others they identify with, on the basis of species, familiarity, shared experiences, relation, etc.

The First Constitution

Let's say that Larry, Mary and Nancy meet to draft a constitution for their Universe. In this constitution they wish to legislate items such as when they may consume crabs for human benefit, given there are a limited number of crabs.

Crab-Induced Blindness and Consumption

There are a few additional facts about this universe that we'll introduce.

Generally, the humans can subsist on vegetation for food. However, crabs play an important role in the human's lives:
1. The humans can randomly go blind, with an unpredictable probability. All they know is that if they do go blind, they will experience 33 units of suffering.
2. Crabs can be consumed two ways, and both options cure blindness:
    a. Crabs can be macerated into a juice, which causes a mere 5 units of $S_{Crab-[n]}$ for a given Crab n, as it causes death near-instantaneously. For humans, while crab juice still serves to cure their blindness, the juice tastes like water and offers 0 Joy units upon consumption.
    b. Crabs can be cooked solid, which causes 100 units of $S_{Crab-[n]}$, and also tastes enjoyable to the human, bringing the human 10 units of $J_{Human-[n]}$. Furthermore, 4 of those units of J_{Human} also manifest as $S_{Distraction}$ (mitigation of suffering) when the human is suffering from blindness at the time of consumption (there is a lag for the curative effect to take hold).
    c. When a human goes blind and then consumes a crab to cure their blindness, the lag time required to procure the crab and for the crab's consumption to have curative effect, causes the human to experience 5 units of suffering (out of the 33 potential suffering units) from blindness before the crab consumption cures the blindness, assuming no $S_{Distraction}$ mitigation.
3. When a crab dies, the other crabs experience a trace amount of empathetic pain toward that crab, of about 1 unit, manifested through the emotional circuits of mourning [26, 27].
    a. We assume that the crabs do not have sophisticated enough cognition to know whether the dead crab was cooked solid (experiencing 100 units of S_{Crab}) or macerated (5 units S_{Crab}), but do feel the pain of the crab's loss (which is an ambiguous mix of their own selfish loss-of-clan and potential empathetic cognizance that the dead crab's disappearance must have entailed non-zero pain while dying).

b. Note that whether or not it is scientifically true that crustaceans have the empathetic capacity inherent in these assumptions, the broader principle of Upsilon Factor optimization still applies, as "crab" could be replaced with "chimpanzee" for example.

Consuming Crabs Recreationally

It is probably already intuitively obvious to the reader that consuming crabs recreationally would not be in the sum benefit of the humans. However, we can prove this using the Snowball, focusing on the Upsilon calculus (which as detailed earlier, precedes any Zeta calculus).

It's helpful to start by analyzing the EWS trade offs for each human involved:

Table 4: Analysis of Action A, Cooking Crab #1 solid, purely for taste, when not blind

Y Factor Effect	Agent: E_{Larry}	Agent: E_{Mary}	Agent: E_{Nancy}
$E_{Agent}WS_{Crab\#1}$	5 (5% * 100 $S_{Crab\#1}$ units)	3 (3% * 100 $S_{Crab\#1}$ units)	3 (3% * 100 $S_{Crab\#1}$ units)
$E_{Agent}WS_{Crabs2-5}$ (Empathy for Other Crabs' Empathetic Pain)	0.15 (5% * 3 * 1 S_{Crab-n} unit)	0.09 (3% * 3 * 1 S_{Crab-n} unit)	0.09 (3% * 3 * 1 S_{Crab-n} unit)
$E_{Agent}WS_{Other-Humans}$ (Empathy for Other Humans' Empathetic Pain)	0.9 (15% E_{Larry} * (E_{Mary}WS + E_{Nancy}WS) from above)	1.35 (15% E_{Mary} * (E_{Larry}WS + 20% $E_{Mary\ of}$ E_{Nancy}WS))	1.35 (15% E_{Nancy} * (E_{Larry}WS + 20% $E_{Nancy\ of}$ E_{Mary}WS))
Effect on Current $S_{Blindness}$	0, N/A	0, N/A	0, N/A
Effect of Future EWS_{Total} from future Blindness risk	Unknown increase in EWS*	Unknown increase in EWS*	Unknown increase in EWS*
$S_{Distraction}$ from $J_{Consumption}$	0, N/A	0, N/A	0, N/A
Effect on $E_{Agent}WS_{Total}$	>6	>4	>4

*Note: Since consuming crabs has no preventative effect on blindness, the effect of consuming a crab is only to reduce the number of crabs available should one of the humans go blind. Since the probability of blindness is not known, and since the availability of crabs after consumption depends on how many crabs have been consumed in the past, there is a fairly complicated calculation with probability assumptions to be made to consider this crab population reduction factor. However, since reducing the number of crabs only increases the probability of unmitigated suffering from blindness, we can assume this leads to only an increase in EWS (demarcated via the 'greater sign' attached to the final Effect on EWS_{Total} numbers).

Table 5: Analysis of Action B, Drinking Crab #1 as juice purely for hydration when not blind

Y Factor Effect	Agent: E_{Larry}	Agent: E_{Mary}	Agent: E_{Nancy}
$EWS_{Crab\#1}$	0.25	0.15	0.15
	(5% * 5)	(3% * 5)	(3% * 5)
$EWS_{Crabs2-5}$	0.15	0.09	0.09
(Empathy for Other Crabs' Empathetic Pain)	(5% * 3)	(3% * 3)	(3% * 3)
$EWS_{Other-Humans}$	~0.03	~0.04	~0.04
(Empathy for Other Humans' Empathetic Pain)	(Same approach as Action A)	(Same approach as Action A)	(Same approach as Action A)
Effect on Current $S_{Blindness}$	0, N/A	0, N/A	0, N/A
Effect of Future EWS_{Total} from future Blindness risk	Unknown increase in EWS*	Unknown increase in EWS*	Unknown increase in EWS*
$S_{Distraction}$ from $J_{Consumption}$	0, N/A	0, N/A	0, N/A
Effect on EWS_{Total}	>0.43	>0.28	>0.28

As Tables 4 and 5 demonstrate, the suffering of the crabs, and the known but difficult-to-measure risk of losing future cures to potential diseases, leads to undesirable EWS evaluations for all 3 observers in both consumption cases. There are differences in the valence between Larry, Mary and Nancy. But the 3 can agree to contractually "outlaw" the non-medicinal consumption of crabs in their universe.

We'll also note that the joy derived from consuming solid cooked crab does not factor into their mutual decision, mostly because there is no distraction offset the joy brings to any relevant suffering in this recreational context. (In a complex analysis, one could identify a separate source of suffering and add nuance to the law in consideration of the consumption of cooked crab to distract a person from that second type of suffering. That separate scenario is out of scope for this simple example analysis however.)

Lastly, the empathetic pain of other humans' empathetic pain did contribute slightly to the calculus, though we used rounded estimates as there is an infinite recursion of empathetic pain that could be calculated and would not significantly change the results. The empathetic pain of the other crabs' pain was not significant, and we may optionally dismiss this factor from further calculations on decision-making in this universe unless there are close decisions involved.

Consuming Crabs Medicinally

A more difficult analysis than the decision of whether to outlaw recreational crab consumption in this universe, is how to legislate medicinal consumption.

Here, the suffering trade offs will require more calculations. To simplify the work, we'll start by ignoring "secondary empathy" effects, e.g. $E_x(E_y(S_z))$, until they need to be invoked to ensure the precise calculations don't tip the decision one way or another.

Since Mary and Nancy are identical in their empathy weightings, we will chart out the trade-offs for the case where Mary is blind and considering consuming crab, and use the same numbers for Nancy, then repeat the chart for the case where Larry is blind.

Table 6: Analysis of Action C, Mary Cooks Crab #1 To Cure Blindness

Y Factor Effect	Observer: E_{Larry}	Observer: E_{Mary}	Observer: E_{Nancy}
$EWS_{Crab\#1}$ + Empathetic Pain for Crab #1 by all other beings (taken from earlier chart)	6	4	4
Curative Effect on Current $EWS_{Mary,Blindness}$	-4.2 (15% * -33 $S_{Blindness}$) + (15% * 5 $S_{Lag\text{-}time}$)	-28 (-(33-5))	-5.6 (20%*(-(33-5)))
Effect of Future EWS_{Total} from future Blindness risk	N/A*	N/A*	N/A*
$EWS_{Distraction}$ from $J_{Consumption}$	-0.6 (15%*-4)	-4	-0.8 (20%*-4)
Effect on EWS_{Total}	1.2	-32	-2.4

*Note: If consensus were built in favor of medicinal use of crabs, then the future need for crabs to address blindness would be irrelevant because there's no reasonable argument for selecting the first instance of blindness vs the fourth instance of blindness to cure in this universe. And if consensus were built against medicinal use of crabs, then their use for curing future blindness would equally be irrelevant. For that reason, we mark this row N/A.

Table 7: Analysis of Action D, Mary Drinks Crab #1 to Cure Blindness

Y Factor Effect	Observer: E_{Larry}	Observer: E_{Mary}	Observer: E_{Nancy}
$EWS_{Crab\#1}$ + Empathetic Pain for Crab #1 by all other beings (taken from earlier chart)	0.43	0.28	0.28
Effect on Current $S_{Mary,Blindness}$	-4.2 (15%*(-(33-5)))	-28 (-(33-5))	-5.6 (20%*(-(33-5)))
Effect of Future EWS_{Total} from future Blindness risk	N/A	N/A	N/A
$EWS_{Distraction}$ from $J_{Consumption}$	0	0	0
Effect on EWS_{Total}	-3.77	-28.28	-5.32

Already, without computing the numbers for Larry's blindness case, we can see that there would be no objection to the consumption of macerated crabs in liquid form as an antidote to blindness. Even if Larry's case were to result in greater total suffering, we intuitively know that Larry's own evaluation of the benefit will be at least as pain-reducing as his evaluation of the benefit for Mary or Nancy is, so he would support it. And since Mary and Nancy would want to support it for themselves, they would need to support it for Larry, at least in order to arrive at unanimous consensus. This conclusion is not strictly true, as we can come up with exceptions where the cost of equality is too great to be worth the benefit to the self, but at least intuitively it's possible to see where the case for liquid medicinal consumption will likely land. We will thoroughly analyze the consensus building options after first examining Larry's consumption case, however.

Table 8: Analysis of Action E, Larry Cooks Crab #1 To Cure Blindness

Y Factor Effect	Observer: E_{Larry}	Observer: E_{Mary}	Observer: E_{Nancy}
$EWS_{Crab\#1}$ + Empathetic Pain for Crab #1 by all other beings (taken from earlier chart)	6	4	4
Effect on Current $S_{Larry,Blindness}$	-28	-4.2 (15%*(-(33-5)))	-4.2 (15%*(-(33-5)))
Effect of Future EWS_{Total} from future Blindness risk	N/A	N/A	N/A
$S_{Distraction}$ from $J_{Consumption}$	-4	-0.6 (15%*-4)	-0.6 (15%*-4)
Effect on EWS_{Total}	**-26**	**-0.8**	**-0.8**

Table 9: Analysis of Action F, Larry Drinks Crab #1 to Cure Blindness

Y Factor Effect	Observer: E_{Larry}	Observer: E_{Mary}	Observer: E_{Nancy}
$EWS_{Crab\#1}$ + Empathetic Pain for Crab #1 by all other beings (taken from earlier chart)	0.43	0.28	0.28
Effect on Current $S_{Larry,Blindness}$	-28	-4.2 (15%*(-(33-5)))	-4.2 (15%*(-(33-5)))
Effect of Future EWS_{Total} from future Blindness risk	N/A	N/A	N/A
$S_{Distraction}$ from $J_{Consumption}$	0	0	0
Effect on EWS_{Total}	**-28.43**	**-4.48**	**-4.48**

Examining Tables 8 and 9, we see that there is no case where the humans would disagree that legalizing the liquid consumption of crab for medicinal purposes would reduce suffering, and therefore the group can agree to legalize it for their universe. (We'll ignore all the intricacies of what legalization actually means, but essentially they can reach consensus that the benefit of medicinal crab maceration outweighs the costs).

When it comes to consuming solid-cooked crab medicinally, there is a difference in perspective for Larry, whose EWS reduces when he is the blindness victim, but increases when either Mary or Nancy are the victim.

It's reasonable to assume Larry could not convince Mary and Nancy to selectively allow medicinal crab cooking only for him, at least not without granting Mary and Nancy the opportunity to selectively draft legislation on other issues in their selfish favor. So consensus could not be reached by all 3 humans that would not unilaterally either allow or disallow this consumption for all 3 humans.

Given this constraint, Larry's math on whether to legalize solid consumption (at least in a vacuum without the alternative option of maceration) would be based on the probability of each potential scenario. Not having any other data, Larry would reasonably assume that there is an equal chance of himself, Mary or Nancy becoming blind. Since he does not know the overall probability of anyone becoming blind, he uses the variable X%, such that P(Mary-Blind) = P(Nancy-Blind) = P(Larry-Blind) = X%.

Larry's probability matrix for all possible scenarios where solid crab might be medicinally eaten becomes:

Table 10: Probability Contribution of Scenarios for Medicinal Solid Crab Consumption

#	Was Mary Blind?	Was Nancy Blind?	Was Larry Blind?	E_{Larry}WS Impact If Solid Crab Is Eaten	P
1	N	N	Y	-26	X%
2	N	Y	N	+1.2	X%
3	N	Y	Y	-24.8	$X\%^2$
4	Y	N	Y	-24.8	$X\%^2$
5	Y	Y	N	+2.4	$X\%^2$
6	Y	Y	Y	-23.6	$X\%^3$

Adding all the rows, the total EWS for Larry among all outcomes is $-24.8(X\%) - 46.2(X\%^2) - 23.6(X\%^3)$. Since all summed coefficients of X^n are negative, and X% is at least 0 making $X^n > 0$, the net effect of legalizing solid crab consumption for Larry's EWS will be to reduce suffering. Thus, in a vacuum, he would be inclined to legalize it alongside Nancy and Mary. If the terms were not all negative, then we could do a more complex calculation involving placeholder values for X to see how the outcome differs based on the probability distribution, and Larry would have to make reasonable guesses as to where between 0-100% X is likely to fall and accordingly make his decision.

While in isolation, each medicinal action of consuming solid or liquid crab would reach consensus between the 3 humans, they might still outlaw solid consumption. Certainly for Larry, there is no situation where solid consumption is preferable to liquid consumption. However, for Mary and Nancy, there is a slight benefit to solid consumption over liquid consumption in the case where they are the victims.

Hypothetical Disagreement

Imagine it were the case that after going through the probability matrix for the medicinal solid-cooked case above, Mary and Nancy were to conclude that solid consumption should be legalized despite the alternative option of liquid consumption, and Larry were to conclude it should not. In that case, the difference of opinion would stem from the distinction in each person's empathy weighting for male humans, female humans, and crabs.

The group would have to first reach consensus on a canonical set of empathy weightings to hold constant, and then could apply those agreed empathy weightings to the decision of solid crab consumption.

One method to reach such a consensus would be to take the average empathy weighting for a given target among all observers, and always apply that empathy weighting to that target when making calculations. This method allows for all decision makers in a society to examine one joint EWS_{Total} score and optimize for Upsilon collectively.

Summary

Naturalism vs Consensus-ism

One question that might be asked of the Upsilon Factor and of the Snowball generally is whether it describes what humans *do*, or what they *should* do, or both, when making decisions. To what degree is it descriptive vs prescriptive?

This work suggests that the Snowball and the Upsilon Factor build on select natural human tendencies, but ignore other natural human tendencies. It does not prescribe that following the selected natural human tendencies (namely of empathy and survival) are "the right thing to do", as a naturalistic argument might suggest.

Instead, this work simply suggests that following those natural tendencies will lead to the *highest consensus among humans* (and arguably the *greatest longitudinal consistency between logic and biological impulse within a human*). Following additional natural tendencies, such as the tendency many have toward being racist, will lead to less consensus. And following fewer natural tendencies (e.g. forsaking empathy and will-to-survive) would be almost impossible for humans to do consistently. So in summary this work proposes that following the Snowball and the Upsilon Factor is what humans should do, *if* they would like to reach maximal social consensus, in the most efficient way possible.

While there could be systems of dogmatic beliefs that humans could be compelled to hold that might lead to consensus among all that are convinced, there would be two issues with relying on dogma to effectuate consensus:

- The first is that almost all systems of dogma end up resulting in self-contradiction (as described in the beginning of this work).
- The second is that dogma does not comport with truth and observable fact.

By acknowledging that humans have a bias toward empathy for the suffering of others, and the neural underpinnings behind this empathy, people can build perspectives on a platform of observational truth that incorporates this scientifically observable bias and seeks to generate consensus by way of shared neural patterns, as opposed to by way of emergent psychological phenomena (like racism and deontological dogma) which are often dispelled by the application of logic and fact.

By reducing all consensus down to the scientific and molecular level, we can create a species-level society that maximizes objectivity and provides a material basis for reasoning about differences in subjective judgements. Thus is the power of the Upsilon Factor.

References

1. Daniel, D. B., & Klaczynski, P. A. (2006). Developmental and Individual Differences in Conditional Reasoning: Effects of Logic Instructions and Alternative Antecedents. In Child Development (Vol. 77, Issue 2, pp. 339–354). Wiley. https://doi.org/10.1111/j.1467-8624.2006.00874.x
2. Brownell, C.A., Iesue, S.S., Nichols, S.R. and Svetlova, M. (2013), Mine or Yours? Development of Sharing in Toddlers in Relation to Ownership Understanding. Child Dev, 84: 906-920. https://doi.org/10.1111/cdev.12009
3. Kim, S., & Harris, P. L. (2014). Belief in Magic Predicts Children's Selective Trust in Informants. In Journal of Cognition and Development (Vol. 15, Issue 2, pp. 181–196). Informa UK Limited. https://doi.org/10.1080/15248372.2012.751917
4. VITIELLO, B., & STOFF, D. M. (1997). Subtypes of Aggression and Their Relevance to Child Psychiatry. In Journal of the American Academy of Child & Adolescent Psychiatry (Vol. 36, Issue 3, pp. 307–315). Elsevier BV. https://doi.org/10.1097/00004583-199703000-00008
5. Macrae, C. N., Milne, A. B., & Bodenhausen, G. V. (1994). Stereotypes as energy-saving devices: A peek inside the cognitive toolbox. Journal of Personality and Social Psychology, 66(1), 37–47. https://doi.org/10.1037/0022-3514.66.1.37
6. Carolyn Parkinson, Walter Sinnott-Armstrong, Philipp E. Koralus, Angela Mendelovici, Victoria McGeer, Thalia Wheatley; Is Morality Unified? Evidence that Distinct Neural Systems Underlie Moral Judgments of Harm, Dishonesty, and Disgust. J Cogn Neurosci 2011; 23 (10): 3162–3180. doi: https://doi.org/10.1162/jocn_a_00017
7. Joshua D. Greene, Joseph M. Paxton. Patterns of neural activity associated with honest and dishonest moral decisions. Proceedings of the National Academy of Sciences Jul 2009, 106 (30) 12506-12511; https://doi.org/10.1073/pnas.0900152106
8. Gintis, H. (2013). Mutualism is only a part of human morality. In Behavioral and Brain Sciences (Vol. 36, Issue 1, pp. 91–91). Cambridge University Press (CUP). https://doi.org/10.1017/s0140525x12000805
9. Boris C. Bernhardt and Tania Singer. The Neural Basis of Empathy. Annual Review of Neuroscience. Vol. 35:1, 1-23. https://doi.org/10.1146/annurev-neuro-062111-150536
10. Stupple, E. J. N., Ball, L. J., Evans, J. S. B. T., & Kamal-Smith, E. (2011). When logic and belief collide: Individual differences in reasoning times support a selective processing model. Journal of Cognitive Psychology, 23(8), 931–941. https://doi.org/10.1080/20445911.2011.589381
11. Daws, R. E., & Hampshire, A. (2017). The Negative Relationship between Reasoning and Religiosity Is Underpinned by a Bias for Intuitive Responses Specifically When Intuition and Logic Are in Conflict. Frontiers in psychology, 8, 2191. https://doi.org/10.3389/fpsyg.2017.02191
12. Reverberi, C., Cherubini, P., Rapisarda, A., Rigamonti, E., Caltagirone, C., Frackowiak, R. S. J., Macaluso, E., & Paulesu, E. (2007). Neural basis of generation of conclusions in

elementary deduction. In NeuroImage (Vol. 38, Issue 4, pp. 752–762). Elsevier BV. https://doi.org/10.1016/j.neuroimage.2007.07.060
13. McCorry L. K. (2007). Physiology of the autonomic nervous system. American journal of pharmaceutical education, 71(4), 78. https://doi.org/10.5688/aj710478
14. Lethality of Suicide Methods. (2017, January 6). Harvard School of Public Health. Retrieved December 30, 2021, from https://www.hsph.harvard.edu/means-matter/means-matter/case-fatality/. (Cited chart from Spicer, R.S. and Miller, T.R. Suicide acts in 8 states: incidence and case fatality rates by demographics and method. American Journal of Public Health. 2000:90(12);1885.)
15. Kelly, D. J., Quinn, P. C., Slater, A. M., Lee, K., Gibson, A., Smith, M., Ge, L., & Pascalis, O. (2005). Three-month-olds, but not newborns, prefer own-race faces. Developmental science, 8(6), F31–F36. https://doi.org/10.1111/j.1467-7687.2005.0434a.x
16. Kurzban, R., & Leary, M. R. (2001). Evolutionary origins of stigmatization: The functions of social exclusion. Psychological Bulletin, 127(2), 187–208. https://doi.org/10.1037/0033-2909.127.2.187
17. Mooney, C., & Viskontas, I. (2014, May 9). The science of your racist brain. Mother Jones. https://www.motherjones.com/politics/2014/05/inquiring-minds-david-amodio-your-brain-on-racism/
18. Workman, C. I., Yoder, K. J., & Decety, J. (2020). The Dark Side of Morality – Neural Mechanisms Underpinning Moral Convictions and Support for Violence. In AJOB Neuroscience (Vol. 11, Issue 4, pp. 269–284). Informa UK Limited. https://doi.org/10.1080/21507740.2020.1811798
19. Slayer rule. (2021, September 21). In Wikipedia. https://en.wikipedia.org/wiki/Slayer_rule
20. Blight, D. Lecture 2 - Southern Society: Slavery, King Cotton, and Antebellum America's "Peculiar" Region. HIST 119: The Civil War and Reconstruction Era, 1845-1877. [Video]. Open Yale Courses. https://oyc.yale.edu/history/hist-119/lecture-2#.
21. Miller, J. G., Xia, G., & Hastings, P. D. (2020). Right Temporoparietal Junction Involvement in Autonomic Responses to the Suffering of Others: A Preliminary Transcranial Magnetic Stimulation Study. In Frontiers in Human Neuroscience (Vol. 14). Frontiers Media SA. https://doi.org/10.3389/fnhum.2020.00007
22. Baskerville, T. A., & Douglas, A. J. (2010). Dopamine and oxytocin interactions underlying behaviors: potential contributions to behavioral disorders. CNS neuroscience & therapeutics, 16(3), e92–e123. https://doi.org/10.1111/j.1755-5949.2010.00154.x
23. Gonzalez-Hernandez, A., & Charlet, A. (2018). Oxytocin, GABA, and TRPV1, the Analgesic Triad?. Frontiers in molecular neuroscience, 11, 398. https://doi.org/10.3389/fnmol.2018.00398
24. Bentham, J. (2007). An introduction to the principles of morals and legislation. Dover Publications.
25. Four Noble Truths. (2021, December 20). In Wikipedia. https://en.wikipedia.org/wiki/Four_Noble_Truths

26. Stelling, T. (2014, March 10). Do lobsters and other invertebrates feel pain? New research has some answers. Washington Post. https://www.washingtonpost.com/national/health-science/do-lobsters-and-other-invertebrates-feel-pain-new-research-has-some-answers/2014/03/07/f026ea9e-9e59-11e3-b8d8-94577ff66b28_story.html
27. T. G. Smith and G. A. Sleno. Do white whales, Delphinapterus leucas, carry surrogates in response to early loss of their young?. Canadian Journal of Zoology. 64(7): 1581-1582. https://doi.org/10.1139/z86-237

Further Reading

The following publications were all useful in the journey of creating this work:

Everett, J. A. C., & Kahane, G. (2020). Switching Tracks? Towards a Multidimensional Model of Utilitarian Psychology. In Trends in Cognitive Sciences (Vol. 24, Issue 2, pp. 124–134). Elsevier BV. https://doi.org/10.1016/j.tics.2019.11.012

Greene J. D. (2007). Why are VMPFC patients more utilitarian? A dual-process theory of moral judgment explains. Trends in cognitive sciences, 11(8), 322–324. https://doi.org/10.1016/j.tics.2007.06.004

Bauman, C. W., McGraw, A. P., Bartels, D. M., & Warren, C. (2014). Revisiting External Validity: Concerns about Trolley Problems and Other Sacrificial Dilemmas in Moral Psychology. In Social and Personality Psychology Compass (Vol. 8, Issue 9, pp. 536–554). Wiley. https://doi.org/10.1111/spc3.12131

Hester, N., & Gray, K. (2020). The Moral Psychology of Raceless, Genderless Strangers. In Perspectives on Psychological Science (Vol. 15, Issue 2, pp. 216–230). SAGE Publications. https://doi.org/10.1177/1745691619885840

Singer, N., Binapfl, J., Sommer, M., Wüst, S., & Kudielka, B. M. (2020). Everyday moral decision-making after acute stress exposure: do social closeness and timing matter? In Stress (pp. 1–6). Informa UK Limited. https://doi.org/10.1080/10253890.2020.1846029

Bates, M. Rats Feel One Another's Pain (2019, April 11). Psychology Today. https://www.psychologytoday.com/us/blog/animal-minds/201904/rats-feel-one-another-s-pain
Related Article: Carrillo, M., Han, Y., Migliorati, F., Liu, M., Gazzola, V., & Keysers, C. (2019). Emotional Mirror Neurons in the Rat's Anterior Cingulate Cortex. In Current Biology (Vol. 29, Issue 8, pp. 1301-1312.e6). Elsevier BV. https://doi.org/10.1016/j.cub.2019.03.024

Kniess, J. (2018). Bentham on animal welfare. In British Journal for the History of Philosophy (Vol. 27, Issue 3, pp. 556–572). Informa UK Limited. https://doi.org/10.1080/09608788.2018.1524746